Tortured mind,
Tortured soul.
Doing what I can,
So I don't lose control.

Trying to overcome,
So that I can live.
While helping others,
Who have nothing more to give.

I would like to dedicate this book to everyone who has been touched in some way by Addiction.

To the addict, please use these poems to help you see what you are doing to yourself and to the people who love you. Use these poems to help you deal with the issues and emotions that you have but don't know how to deal with. While reading these poems, seek treatment to help you deal with the emotions that you are experiencing.

To everyone else, please use this book as a guide to help better understand what is going on inside the mind of an addict. They are not bad people. Depending on their addiction, they can go unnoticed for many years. But in the end, there are going to be underlying issues from their addiction. Some issues were the reason for the addiction, while others were caused by the addiction.

Joseph Howard

PRINCESS IN THE NIGHT

AUSTIN MACAULEY PUBLISHERS™
LONDON • CAMBRIDGE • NEW YORK • SHARJAH

Ordering Information:
Quantity sales: special discounts are available on quantity purchases by corporations, associations, and others. For details, contact the publisher at the address below.

Publisher's Cataloging-in-Publication data
Howard, Joseph
Princess in the Night

ISBN 9781645363675 (Paperback)
ISBN 9781645363682 (Hardback)
ISBN 9781645369004 (ePub e-book)

Library of Congress Control Number: 2020906263

www.austinmacauley.com/us
First Published (2020)
Austin Macauley Publishers LLC
40 Wall Street, 28th Floor
New York, NY 10005
USA

mail-usa@austinmacauley.com
+1 (646) 5125767

I would like to add a special thank you to my friend and Artist
Heike E. Becker.

Table of Content

First, I would like to thank everyone for buying the book.
This book cost me more than just the last year of my life, this book almost killed me.
I know that you may think that this is an exaggeration, but it is not.
I am an extremely emotional man. Sometimes this is a blessing or a gift, other times it feels more like a curse.
I experience emotions so deeply that it affects my entire life. There were times in this past year when I was unable to move, curled up in a ball on the floor. These poems were my therapy to help myself through one of the most devastating times of my life. I lived through everything that is written here in this book. I know they say that what doesn't kill you makes you stronger. In my case, it's not true. My life has been destroyed a couple of times in the past. Each time the recovery has been harder than the time before. I fear the time when I will not be able to recover and be lost forever in my pain.

People like to believe that men should be stoic and unemotional. Even though most men generally try to not show it, we feel emotions the same as everyone else.

From the time I was a small child, I always felt that I had a guardian angel watching over me. It must have been my guardian angel that sent me a beautiful angel to save me. If it was not for this angel, I would not be here today to finish this book. We all have our demons from our past. Some extremely powerful demons lurk in the back of everyone's mind. Do we give into them? Or do we fight them?
Each person has to decide this for themselves. If your demon is, or someone you know has the demon of addiction? This is the most powerful demon I have ever encountered. It can make parents sacrifice their own children. It can take someone you love very dearly, a wonderful happy person, and turn them into a demon themselves. All we can do is offer love, guidance and support their efforts to get clean. When it comes down to it, it has to be their choice to want to get clean and stay clean. Otherwise, you are fighting a demon that you will never be able to win against. Sometimes this demon's

hold on the ones we love is so strong, all we can do is walk away to protect ourselves. This is so hard to do, I know. Only a few of us will be lucky enough to see our loved ones realize there is a better life waiting for them on the other side of addiction. Unfortunately, too many of our loved ones will end up succumbing to this Demon.

May they rest in peace and find forgiveness.

Princess in the Night

I have walked in the darkness, too many years.
Fighting the demons, that scream in my ears.

I carry a torch, to help me find my way.
I fear how long, in the darkness I must stay.

The darkness within my mind.
My demons from past time.

A torch of hope, to fight them back.
The demons never ceasing, ready to attack.

My light of love, that was self made.
Over time this light, had started to fade.

As my light was fading, the darker it became.
The demons come closer, I am going insane.

As I brace for the battle, over who I will be.
I see a light, slowly coming towards me.

A light of love, that is fading like mine.
The closer it came, my light started to shine.

It is you in the darkness, with your fading light.
That ignites my love, and brightens the fight.

We come together, and fight side by side.
The demons that haunt us, slowly subside.

Our lights grow stronger, with every hour.
Our love is growing, like a beautiful flower.

Together we stand, our light now so bright.
No darkness around, only beauty and light.

You saved me from the darkness, and brought back the light.
I will love you forever, My Princess in the Night.

My love, my life, my everything. I love you more than you will ever know.
You saved me from myself.
I love you so much. My Princess in the Night.

Joseph A. Howard
03/23/2018

I dedicate this poem to the woman I love
My Princess in the Night.

The Future

Up to this point we have walked alone, too often being led astray.
We come together on an unknown path, let us try to find our way.

Take my hand and walk with me, down future's path together.
We hope and pray the love we find, will somehow last forever.

It will not be easy, to keep our love so strong.
To our torch of love, we hold on tight, as we carefully move along.

We forcefully declare to all around, our love is here to stay!
We look to a future, of being together, our love will show us the way.

The future is still unwritten, there is nothing for us to see.
We look into each other's eyes, a love that's meant to be.

With each step our love will grow, and guide us on our way.
We walk together for many years, so thankful for each day.

We hold onto each other's hand, with a love so full of life.
We stop one day and I kneel down, to ask you to be my wife.

The day will come when I must go, and walk into the light.
But never fear, I'll be waiting there, My Princess in the Night.

Joseph A. Howard
03/28/2018

I dedicate this poem to the woman I love.
I will love you forever

Demons of the Past

Confusion is controlling me, it's driving me insane.
I don't know how to deal with this, this constant loving pain.

Love should not hurt so much, this should be a hopeful time.
The pain is ever present, not sure that you are mine.

The past is a demon, always spreading evil doubt.
Everything it's telling me, makes me want to shout.

My insecurity is rising, I don't know your love is real.
The only thing I know for sure, is how you make me feel.

I am trying to be honest here, to let you know the truth.
Everything must come to light, to remove the demon's tooth.

I do not want to know the past, I need to know the now.
The past it seems cannot be changed, but the future? Only how?

My mind is always running wild, I don't know what to do.
My heart just keeps telling me, there is no one else but you.

To know for sure that you love me too, will help me win this fight.
Please show me I'm the only one, My Princess in the Night.

Joseph A. Howard
04/01/2018

I dedicate this poem to the only one for me.
My love, my life, my Princess in the Night.

We Stand Alone

All the lies and stories, that people have told.
Never ending confusion, and being so cold.

What people have said, about you and me.
If the truth doesn't matter, please just let us be.

The lies they tell, to cover their asses.
As we burn to the ground, nothing but ashes.

Nobody cares, what the truth might be.
Pain and suffering, is all they want to see.

We have each other, we know what is real.
Attacked by everyone, there's no time to heal.

No one believes us, though we try to explain.
The truth doesn't matter, we enjoy your pain.

It is you and me, alone together.
Against the world, now and forever.

The truth untold, no one caring what's right.
We stand alone, My Princess in the Night.

Joseph A. Howard
04/02/2018

I dedicate this poem to the woman I love.
Stay strong, my princess.
We don't need them, only each other.

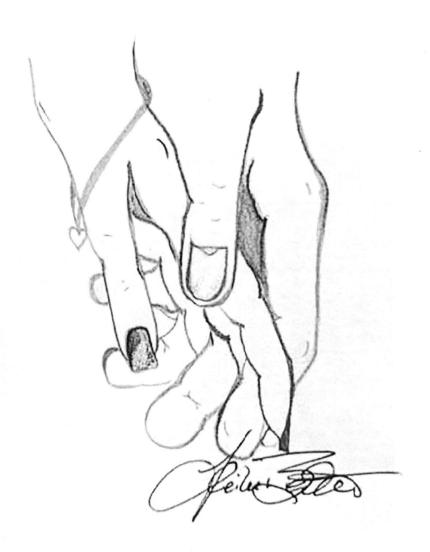

Vows

If we write our own vows, this would be mine.
I will love you forever, until the end of time.

When I see the sparkle, bright in your eyes.
The love that I feel, should be no surprise.

Love can be fleeting, unless it is true.
For now and forever, mine is for you.

To have and to hold, for now and forever.
A bond so strong, that no one can sever.

With a love so pure, it has never felt so right.
I see it in your eyes, when I hold you at night.

My heart just melts, with every touch.
All I can say, is I love you so much.

When I take my hand, and caress your cheek.
My body goes numb, and my legs get weak.

I feel so much love, when you are around.
When I try to speak, I can't make a sound.

With a life full of love, and a love full of life.
I would love it so much, to call you my wife.

With every ending, there is a new beginning.
In the game of life, we should always be winning.

No more being single, it's time to say I DO.
I have no regrets, because I am marring you.

So toss the bouquet, and let it take flight.
Together forever, My Princess in the Night.

Joseph A. Howard
04/03/2018

I dedicate this poem to my one and only love,
You are my soul mate.

I hope real soon to say I DO.
All my love, it's only for you.

Forgiveness

The choices we've made, the things we have done.
We must live with forever, they cannot be undone.

The forgiving is not easy, forgetting is even harder.
We have both been hurt, the how doesn't matter.

Forgiving ourselves, as well as each other.
Just how is the thing, that we must discover.

Forgiving each other, will take some time.
Rebuilding our trust, is a hill we must climb.

To see what we've done, is so hard to face.
Forgiving ourselves, must also take place.

Not by our choices, it is more like a feeling.
We reach for the stars, not just the ceiling.

Our love for each other, is pulling us together.
It's written in the stars, a love meant forever.

With love in our hearts, all can be conceived.
With forgiveness our future, will be achieved.

Our love can bring forgiveness, each and every day.
Soon we'll be together, and both come home to stay.

Love can be so hard, but that won't last forever.
Nothing can stop us, if we want to be together.

As we ask for forgiveness, we must hold each other tight.
For our future together, My Princess in the Night.

Joseph A. Howard
04/04/2018

I dedicate this poem to the woman I love.

Please forgive me as I have forgiven you.

Faith

Sometimes in the future, we will struggle for our wealth.
We will always have each other, if not for so much else.

The struggles we will face, can seem so very hard.
Often it will feel, like our path is being bard.

We put our trust in God, as well as in each other.
His plan for our future, this we must discover.

The path where he will lead us, to us is yet unknown.
If we walk with his love, we will never walk alone.

Discovering this path, that he is leading us along.
Believing in his love, nothing can go wrong.

Just knowing that his love, can forgive us of our sin.
He purified our souls, so our new life can begin.

As we walk along his path, we will always walk together.
Our hearts so filled with love, we pray it lasts forever.

Hand in hand we go, as we discover this love for us.
We follow in his guiding light, our faith is our big plus.

For our love to stay so strong, we must always do what's right.
Faith in our Father's love, My Princess in the Night.

Joseph A. Howard
04/08/2018
I dedicate this poem to my love, my life, my future wife.
My Princess in the Night.

Fear

I'm afraid of you, I'm afraid of me.
I close my eyes, I'm afraid to see.

I'm afraid of everything, is it a lie? Can it be real?
I just do not know, what I'm supposed to feel?

I'm afraid if it's the truth, and I'm afraid that it's a lie.
Sometimes I get this feeling, that I wish that I could die.

If I did not feel the love, then I guess I wouldn't care.
With a love as strong as mine, it will always be right there.

I'm afraid of this love, I'm afraid of my whole life.
All this fear can kill me, it's as deadly as a knife.

I'm afraid to sleep, I'm afraid to stay awake.
I don't know how much, my heart can even take.

Yes my fear is increasing, with every single day.
I feel that you keep slipping, farther and farther away.

Yes I fear the day, when you will not be there.
My heart so full of pain, nothing but despair.

I am alone and afraid, don't take away love's light.
I'm afraid of the darkness, My Princess in the Night.

Joseph A Howard
04/10/2018
I dedicate this poem to the love of my life.
My Princess in the Night

This poem is but a memory
From a long time ago.

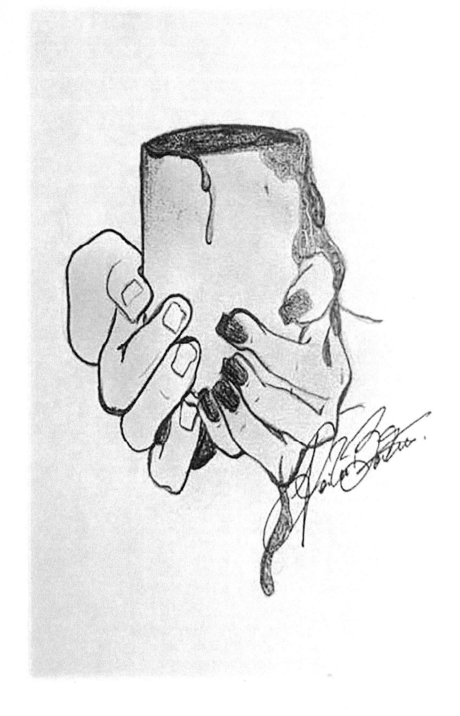

Hope

Sometimes it's a struggle, sometimes it's a delight.
We look towards the future, oh, what a beautiful sight.

We picture in our minds, all the wonders that can be.
The blessings of tomorrow, all laid out for us to see.

The promise of a future, cannot be guaranteed.
Trusting in each other, we carefully plant that seed.

The dreaming and the scheming, everything that we do.
We pray for a new tomorrow, have faith it will come true.

It will not always be easy, to find it every day.
As we think about the future, our love is here to stay.

They say it springs eternal, never ending, don't give up.
As we smile at each other, holding that overflowing cup.

To have it is believing, that everything will be OK.
We try to find the spark, to help us find our way.

As we pray for our future, we hold each other tight.
Hope is all we have sometimes, My Princess in the Night.

Joseph A. Howard
04/11/2018

I dedicate this poem to my future wife, "I Hope"

May hope guide us along our path,
And we always are able to find it.

Departure

Although things might seem, quite hopeless right now.
You know you'll survive, you just do not know how.

It's hard to be going, not knowing what's to come.
With the love of your friends, you know you'll overcome.

Keep us in your prayers, for the time you are away.
Those who are your friends, will think of you each day.

Many letters will be written, so that we can keep in touch.
Remember that we care, and will miss you very much.

The time will come, when you come back home.
Our letters to assure you, you were never left alone.

Some loved ones may be gone, and new ones have arrived.
Once you feel the love, you'll be so happy you survived.

There will be some people, who will hold on to a grudge.
If they can't find forgiveness, then who are we to judge?

Helpless is not hopeless, your future is still so bright.
From all of us who love you, your Princess in the Night.

Joseph A. Howard
04/16/2018

I dedicate this poem to friends that must move on.
Although you are leaving, you will never be gone.
You will always be in our hearts.
We will miss you.

We Believe

We believe, what we want to believe.
To change a mind, is hard to achieve.

We believe sometimes, things can go wrong.
We will have to endure, but just for how long?

We believe first impressions, cannot be undone.
To show them the truth, this battle is hard won.

We believe in the future, things will get better.
When we express our love, in every letter.

We believe that tomorrow, we will start anew.
That somehow our dreams, will always come true.

We believe in each other, to do what is right.
To strengthen our love, and brighten the fight.

We believe that the truth, can finally set us free.
To express our love, so that everyone can see.

We believe in the love, we have for each other.
Our future together, we soon will uncover.

We believe that some things, are just worth the fight.
I believe in you, My Princess in the Night.

Joseph A. Howard
04/19/2018

I dedicate this poem to my only true love.
I believe that I love you
I believe in our future
I believe in you

Not Alone

I hide behind the feeling, that I am all alone.
Built up walls around me, and hide behind the stone.

Not allowing myself to love, it's easier to hide away.
I don't believe I deserve it? True love is not my way.

Afraid to face the future, still hiding from the past.
Don't put your faith in me, this love can never last.

To be loved is one thing, feeling the love? Quite another.
We must open up our hearts, fully trusting in each other.

It's hard for me to remember, it has been so long a time.
To find my love and set it free, and trust that you are mine.

Putting everything behind me, to see what may come next.
Letting go of the past, to feel our love's effect.

The future is always coming, no way to slow it down.
It helps to know you love me? And will always be around.

I hope so much your love is real, I don't want to be afraid.
Is this my dream come true? For what I've always prayed?

Time to take a leap of faith, and let the love come in.
Feeling everything I feel, let's let our love begin.

Feeling your love cannot be wrong, I am feeling it tonight.
Remember you are not alone, your Princess in the Night.

Joseph A. Howard
04/21/2018
I dedicate this poem to everyone, we all have a past.
We all deserve love and forgiveness.

Addiction

My addiction is a demon, much more powerful than me.
This demon is my master, so please just let us be.

I want so much to end it all, I can't take this anymore.
Just hand me my needle, then walk right out the door.

Please don't try to help me, for some it never works.
If you get in to its way, you will end up getting hurt.

This addiction is killing me, I know that this is true.
If you do not runaway, this demon will hurt you too.

This demon is controlling me, it's will I must obey.
I have asked that you please walk away, why do you choose to stay?

Do not come with all your love, I just don't want to feel.
Love will always go away, my wounds will never heal.

Why do you choose to give your love, it cannot fix the pain.
If you think your love can heal, you are just insane.

Every time I try to fight, it will come back even stronger.
Please just let me die, so I can't hurt you any longer.

Recovery is for others, for me there's no way back.
This demon will always find me, and then he will attack.

Why won't you just give up now, and leave us all alone.
The demon lives inside me, I am its only home.

I no longer have the strength to fight, this demon every day.
You say that you will not give up, to help me find a way.

You say that you love me, you don't want to see me die.
I tell you that I love you too, I don't want to see you cry.

You promise to be here for me, to help me one more time.
I feel I'm not worth your love, you tell me you are mine.

I would sacrifice my life for you, to help you win this fight.
You are worth all my love, My Princess in the Night.

Joseph A. Howard
04/25/2018

I dedicate this poem to the love of my life.

I thank the Lord every day that you are still here to read this.

Doubt

Doubt is a demon, always creeping in your mind.
Once its seed is planted, everything will unwind.

Is this real, is this true, to question everything you do?
Never ask if it isn't true, you can only trust what I tell you.

Look for truth and watch for lies, you're never really sure.
Some suspicion will always be, to ensure you're insecure.

The demon of doubt is a tricky one, it doesn't always lie.
Often it will tell some truth, with deception still close by.

This demon seldom works alone, it uses others too.
They pretend to be your friends, then tell you it's all true.

To sow the seeds of deception, planting jealousy and fear.
His voice always whispering, things you don't want to hear.

Lies or truth you will not know, until it is too late.
The battle rages in your mind, is it choice or is it fate?

This demon's always plotting, you never know what's right.
To overcome we must believe, My Princess in the Night.

Joseph A. Howard
04/26/2018

I dedicate this poem, to the only one that matters.
Doubt comes in, when our love has been shattered.
We pick up the pieces, start putting it back together.
Devotion is the key, for our love to last forever.

I love you
As demons go, this one is bad, it comes as a friend, but then you've been had.

Addiction and Love

To be in love with an addict, is not an easy thing to do.
For this love to have a chance, make sure that it is true.

The constant lies they will tell, to hide what they have done.
Trying to find forgiveness, so your love won't be undone.

You can never really be sure, of what is truly going on.
Overdose is on your mind, so afraid when they are gone.

You're in love with the person, while you hate their addiction.
You pray every day, for some kind of interdiction.

There will always be times, when you want to give it up.
But your love is so strong, you can't think of breaking up.

When things get out of control, you feel like you are lost.
You cling to your love, no matter what this love might cost.

Why do we love them? No one can know for sure.
It is just something we feel, for love there is no cure.

Doubt and denial, will become your closest friends.
To be in love with an addict, and pray it never ends.

Love can be an addiction, controlling in its own right.
I will love you forever, My Princess in the Night.

Joseph A. Howard
04/27/2018

I dedicate this poem to all those who love someone with a problem.
I do know how you feel.
I love you My Princess in the Night.

I See

I see the pain and suffering, hiding in your heart.
I see all the love, that is tearing you apart.

I see all the battles, that you have endured.
I see all the scars, and the pain that has occurred.

I see the confusion, running through your mind.
I see all the things, that keep you so entwined.

I see your compassion, that makes other people smile.
I see that you've been struggling, with your demons for a while.

I see it in your eyes, and hear it in your voice.
I see that you feel, that you had no other choice.

I see a lot of things, that you don't want to believe.
I see all the goodness, that's why I cannot leave.

I see a heart of gold, that has faded just a bit.
I see that you've been struggling, to make sense of all of it.

I see in your heart, the stories you will not tell.
I see that you feel, life has cast an evil spell.

I see all your efforts, to try and make things right.
I see my future with you, My Princess in the Night.

Joseph A. Howard
05/07/2018
I dedicate this poem to my love and my life.
I see so much, My Princess in the Night.

I see you, you see me.
Our love is meant to be.

Devotion

Devotion is not an emotion; it is a commitment that we choose.
We must guard it very close, for it is something we can lose.

It means always knowing, that we will never give it up.
Trusting in each other, never thinking to break up.

We must always be faithful, placing trust in one another.
To keep our love alive, it must only be for each other.

There can be no one else, that comes between you and me.
Not even the closest friend, or even harder, our family.

Because it is a choice, that is supported by a feeling.
We must always work to keep it, no chance that it starts failing.

There will be times, when it is the hardest thing to keep.
When you do not feel the love, your devotion can get weak.

Knowing that you love me, strengthens my devotion.
I never get the feeling, you are lacking in emotion.

Our devotion to each other, might cause others to be shattered.
Putting no one else before me, makes me feel like our love matters.

My devotion is forever, until the end of time.
My heart is so full of love, just knowing you are mine.

Things don't always start out right, a struggle from the start.
We somehow find the will to fight, somewhere inside our heart.

No matter what may come for us, we will always win the fight.
Devotion to each other, My Princess in the Night.
Joseph A. Howard
05/17/2018
I dedicate this poem, with all of my emotions.
To the woman that I love, you strengthen my devotion.

Regret

Some things that we do, we will live to regret.
A second chance at life, only a few will get.

Some time to think? I now have plenty.
If I could turn back the years, I'd go back twenty.

Back to a time, before my life took a bad turn.
So many bridges I've crossed, I wish now I could burn.

I sit here every day, and think about the past.
I don't know for how long, I hope that I can last.

They can't keep me forever, is what I tell myself.
As I look at my calendar, sitting up on the shelf.

I mark another day, they are now running all together.
The time goes so slowly, it seems like its forever.

I've hurt someone I love, I know what I have done.
I pray for forgiveness, please make it all undone.

I am feeling so alone, overcome by all my shame.
I did this I know, there is no one else to blame.

From God above, forgiveness is now mine.
From my love now too, but this one took some time.

The not knowing is the worst, how long it will be.
I believe for my future, my love may hold the key.

I regret what I've done, still trying to make things right.
My future is with you my love, your Princess in the Night.

Joseph A. Howard
05/26/2018

Moments

There will be moments, we will never forget.
Some good, some bad, and others we regret.

The good moments we have, we hold within our hearts.
So we can always be together, even when were apart.

To keep our love so strong, good moments become memories.
When things start getting hard, these memories are the remedies.

To be able to see the good times, the bad are needed as well.
If you don't have the bad times? How could you even tell?

The bad times while painful, teach us lessons that we need.
To become a better person, we sometimes have to bleed.

Some moments we remember, are the ones we live to regret.
To realize what we've done, and know we'll never forget.

When we hurt the ones we love, are the worst moments of our fall.
But the moments of forgiveness, are the best moments of them all.

A split second in time, forever burned into our sight.
Some moments last forever, My Princess in the Night.

Joseph A. Howard
05/29/2018

Tender moments in time, when you let your love shine.
Are the moments that let me know, that you are truly mine.
I LOVE YOU
I dedicate this poem to the woman I fell in love with,

The very first moment I saw her.
May our good moments always outnumber the bad.

Worth Fighting For

There are things in life, worth fighting for.
The people we love, and so much more.

To live a life, filled with happiness and love.
We fight all our demons, with help from above.

The battle will be hard, never ending it may seem.
As the battle rages on, even fighting in our dream.

We see everything we have, and all we stand to lose.
We find the will to fight, so we never have to choose.

We have made up our minds, we are never going back.
When the demon gets too close, we are so ready to attack.

It no longer can control us, we say it every day.
The future is ours to live, not it's to take away.

As the battle continues on, we will stand our ground and fight.
Some things are just worth fighting for, My Princess in the Night.

Joseph A. Howard
05/30/2018

I dedicate this poem to the woman that I love.
I would fight every day for you.

You are worth fighting for.

Time

The time is getting nearer, when things will be getting better.
The troubles of the past, just memories in a letter.

For our future to begin, a little patience is all we need.
We must wait a little more, to make sure that we succeed.

The next step in our journey, will be coming very fast.
We plan for our future, to make sure that it will last.

Time to see is all we need, to make sure our love will grow.
From the seeds we have planted, our future we'll soon know.

Everything we've started, will take a bit more time.
To make sure that it is ready, before our love can shine.

With tenderness and love, our future will start to flow.
The love that we have planted, soon will begin to show.

The future of our hearts, will grow stronger in love's light.
Time and love is what we need, My Princess in the Night.

Joseph A. Howard
05/31/2018

I dedicate this poem to the woman I love.

My love for you is timeless.
Time to hurt, Time to heal, Time to forgive, Time to feel
And the most important time of all,
Time to LOVE

Pieces

The pieces of our shattered dreams, everything destroyed.
The sharp and jagged edges, are something to avoid.

Frantically searching, we hope to find, the pieces of our hearts.
As we sort through all the pieces, we are saving the best parts.

We take some pieces from our past, start putting them back together.
We take our time and rearrange, this time it must last forever.

The pieces we can always change, if we don't like what we see.
The life that we are building, broken pieces of you and me.

We changed some things, and added new, to make it so much stronger.
We commit ourselves, to each other, no more hiding any longer.

Our faith and trust will grow each day, this we will discover.
A new beginning, built on love, with devotion to each other.

Our future is like a puzzle, putting all the pieces in their place.
I know it must be going right, I see a smile on your face.

In the future things will change, some pieces replaced by others.
This puzzle is always growing, building a new life for each other.

Taking from our broken dreams, to build our future right.
Broken pieces from both of us, My Princess in the Night.

Joseph A. Howard
06/07/2018

I dedicate this poem to the best pieces of our love. Sometimes things have to break, before you can see where it was weak. We pick up all the pieces, to start building something sweet. There are pieces of you inside of me, and pieces of me inside of you. Together we can make it, something better and brand new.

Home

When the sun comes up in the morning, its light slowly fills the skies.
I see you sleeping next to me, I just can't believe my eyes.

This must be a dream, this can't be real, it has been so long a time.
My beautiful love, are you really here? This must be all in my mind.

I think that I am having a dream, I don't want to get out of bed.
Please open your eyes, so I can see, this isn't all in my head.

I lie in bed and watch you sleep, there's so much I want to say.
A feeling of love from head to toe, please never go away.

I don't want to go, but I know I must, it's time to start the day.
I slip out of bed, to quietly leave, it's so hard to walk away.

I stop for a moment to watch you sleep, before I leave the room.
So sweet you are, while you're asleep, the sun will be rising soon.

Wake up my love, you are finally home, let's start this life off right.
With a loving kiss, you open your eyes, My Princess in the Night.

Joseph A. Howard
06/12/2018

I dedicate this poem to the woman I love,
You are finally home, please never go away again.
Life without you has been a nightmare.
I love you so much, my beautiful Princess.
I missed you so much.

Starting Over

Starting over isn't easy, so many things we must redo.
The love we share is there, everything else we build anew.

The rebuilding will not be easy, so many bumps along the way.
With love and devotion, in our hearts, we will always find a way.

Some bumps will seem like mountains, too big to climb alone.
Within our hearts, we will find, a way to build our home.

The biggest problems we will face, will come from our own mind.
To overcome these issues, we must share them when it's time.

We cannot change, when we do not know, how we've hurt each other.
The anger and pain, we hide inside, to start healing we must uncover.

We share our thoughts and listen too, to work through all the fear.
A lot of things that will be said, are things we don't want to hear.

We have to face what we have done, bringing everything into the light.
Starting over isn't easy, My Princess in the Night.

Joseph A. Howard
06/18/2018

I dedicate this poem to the woman I want to start over with.

My love, starting over will mean some work.
I am willing to do whatever it takes to have a happy life with you.
I love you so much, My Princess in the Night.

One Day at A Time

Every morning when we open our eyes, we look around to see.
All the love that gives us strength, flowing between you and me.

We live each day one day at a time, and take whatever may come.
Good or bad, easy or hard, for our future we overcome.

Our strength comes from the love we have, we feel this every day.
To make a better tomorrow, our love will show us the way.

We get out of bed to face the day, knowing our love is strong.
We say a prayer to God above, so that nothing will go wrong.

As the day unfolds, we will see, with love everything gets better.
We trust our love to give us strength, so thankful were together.

As night time comes and we look back, we know we did survive.
We climb into bed at the end of the day, so thankful were alive.

With faith in God and in each other, we know we'll win this fight.
One day at a time is all we can do, My Princess in the Night.

Joseph A. Howard
06/20/2018
I dedicate this poem to the woman I want to spend every day with.
One day at a time, turns into a week, then a month, and then a year.
One day at a time until the end of time.
I will love you forever.

Frozen

I feel as if I am frozen, stuck in time and space.
Waiting for an answer, I do not want to face.

My mind has been shattered, stuck in a single thought.
Destruction is all around me, I'm frozen and distraught.

To be frozen in one place in time, you can feel your heart just drop.
You wish you could just close your eyes, you want this pain to stop.

Your blood runs cold and your eyes are burning, at everything you see.
Your perfect love, your perfect life, how could this ever be?

To see the love you held so close, be shattered before your eyes.
This frozen feeling that I feel, should be no big surprise.

Betrayed by the one you love, you are living your biggest fear.
Frozen by what others say, things you don't want to hear.

Time will tell if this love we have, will ever be worth this fight.
I am frozen here waiting for you, My Princess in the Night.

Joseph A. Howard
06/25/2018

I dedicate this poem to you my princess.

My love, my life has been frozen.
Will you come back and thaw me out?
I feel so cold, too much pain. I don't want this life anymore.
I am sorry, I just love you so much.
Forgive me, I just don't want to live without you.

Help

As I lie in my bed, and try to fall asleep.
It's my mind I fear, and the secrets that I keep.

The things I have tried, to forget ever happened.
They come into my mind, I feel so abandoned.

Things from my past, that are destroying my mind.
I don't know how to deal, I can't leave it behind.

I cry out for help, there's no one that can hear.
The silence is deafening, increasing my fear.

Help me please, I no longer want to live.
I have nothing left, nothing left to give.

There is no way out, it is all in my head.
Forever being haunted, until I am dead.

No escape from myself, how long can I last.
Not being able, to forgive my own past.

The things I have done, would scare you away.
I hide everything, because I want you to stay.

I don't want to hurt you, I wish you would go.
My past is so bad, I don't want you to know.

Please stay with me, I love you so much.
I hate that you love me, I can't stand your touch.

I am no good, I wish you would see.
Why must I love you? What's wrong with me?

The things I have done, you will never forget.
If I ever let you in, that's something you'll regret.

No one can love me, with all that I've done.
There's way too much, for you to overcome.

In the end when you know, you will hurt me too.
Just like every other man, who said "I love you".

The pain is not worth it, I no longer want to fight
No one can help me, your Princess in the Night.

Joseph A. Howard
07/06/2018

I dedicate this poem to you my princess.
Sometimes I think that this is how you feel.
I don't care about the past, I only care about the future.

What I Can See

I wish you could see, what I can see.
The love that's inside, please find the key.

The key to being happy, the key to our new life.
Please unlock your heart, and say you'll be my wife.

My wife for now, and my life forever.
This love we share, I will always treasure.

Treasure the moments, that we will create.
The moments of love, that others might hate.

Others might hate, the love we have found.
They will wish that theirs, could be so profound.

Profound and determined, our love is emerging.
For something so pure, others keep searching.

Searching for the love, that's expressed by a ring.
We pray for our future, even after everything.

After everything, our love will be even stronger.
We've sacrificed so much, though our future we must ponder.

Ponder how we go on, for our love is meant to be.
Our desire to stay together, is all what I can see.

What I can see, is worth so much more.
Just believe in yourself, and open up the door.

The door to a new life, so beautiful and bright.
I wish you could see what I can see, My Princess in the Night.

Joseph A. Howard
07/14/2018

I dedicate this poem to you my love.
What I can see?
A future full of love, between you and me.
I love you

Believe In Me

Believe in me, that I will do what is right.
To protect our love, I am ready to fight.

Anyone who tries, to come between you and me.
They will soon learn, they should have let us be.

Believe in me, because nothing else matters.
I will find the ones, who left us in tatters.

I no longer care, who I might have to hurt.
If they get in my way, I will grind them into dirt.

Believe in me, I have planned this all out.
I know what to do, and what it's all about.

The time has come, to be more aggressive.
To take control, but not be obsessive.

Believe in me, I will do what I must.
When I am done, we will know who to trust.

Not everyone is a friend, who wants what is best.
I will destroy the evil, and help all the rest.

Believe in me, I will save all I can.
To figure out who? is now my new plan.

All who are good, I will vigorously defend.
The ones, who are evil, will soon meet their end.

Believe in me, I will never tell you a lie.
The time has come, all evil must die.

I must do the things, that I think are right.
To protect you my love, My Princess in the Night.

Joseph A. Howard
07/16/2018

I dedicate this poem to you my love.
My love, sometimes a man needs to do what a man needs to do.
If not? he is not a man.

So Alone

I feel so alone, when I cannot hear your voice.
The emptiness I feel, was never by my choice.

When you pulled away, a pain shot through my heart.
Then everything inside me, started falling apart.

My love is still within me, I just cannot grab a hold.
When I reach to feel you, all I'm feeling is the cold.

I'm missing you my love, it's hurting me so much.
I try so hard to heal, but I miss your tender touch.

The pain that I am feeling, in my heart it's always there.
Sometimes I think this pain, is way too much to bear.

The thought of life without you, crushing me every day.
My heart is bleeding on my soul, this cannot be our way.

Our story is of love, it is not one of goodbye.
I beg of you my Princess, don't let our love just die.

I want for us to take the time, to make everything all right.
My love for you is still so strong, My Princess in the Night.

Joseph A. Howard
07/18/2018

I dedicate this poem, to our story untold.
No more feeling alone, let's heat up the cold.

Overcome

To truly overcome, I must put it all behind.
Forgiving all that happened, to clear it from my mind.

This isn't ever easy, but it's something I must do.
Overcoming all that happened, is something I do for you.

My mind is overloaded, trying to figure this all out.
Every time there's something new, your love I start to doubt.

Enough is enough, I can't take it anymore, please just stop the pain.
My mind is shouting that's too much, any more and I'll go insane.

The mind is something fragile, sometimes it can even break.
If I try to go too fast, can be more than it can take.

Some things that I must overcome, are things that really matter.
Trying to understand it all, can cause my mind to shatter.

It takes some time to understand, then forgive and overcome.
Moving too fast can risk it all, this battle so hard won.

In my mind there is a battle, a raging bloody fight.
In the end I will overcome, My Princess in the Night.

Joseph A. Howard
07/24/2018

I dedicate this poem to you my love,
To everything that we've overcome.
May our future be much better.
We strive each day to just hold on.
And just keep it all together.
Better together
I love you

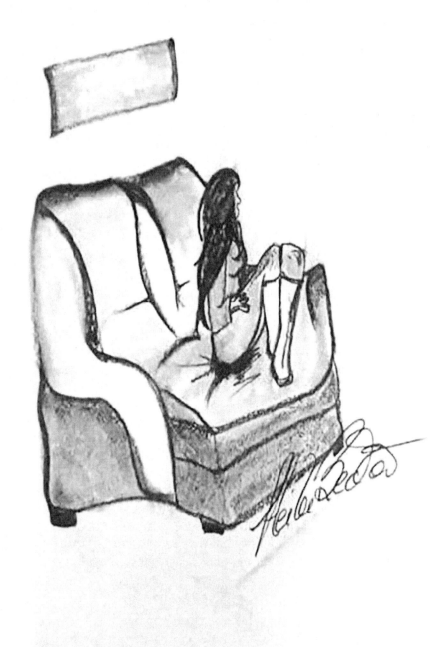

Belong

My dearest love, I wish you would see.
That I belong to you, and you belong to me.

The feeling of belonging, brings security and love.
Belonging to each other, is knowing you're beloved.

When you walk, through the house, and your heart is filled with peace.
You sit down, on the couch, and all your troubles cease.

You know that this is right, you've known this all along.
Now it's time, for you to see, that this is where you belong.

You feel it in your heart, and you know it in your mind.
Our souls have been together, since the universe combined.

You know that I love you, more than anything in this life.
I have asked you many times, won't you please become my wife.

Your future is with me, with a devotion that lasts forever.
It's the destiny of our love, we are meant to be together.

If you need a little proof, that we are meant to last.
Just look into your heart, to our future not the past.

When you look all around, and it all just feels so right.
Then you know where you belong, My Princess in the Night.

Joseph A. Howard
07/25/2018

I dedicate this poem to the woman who my heart belongs to.
We belong to our future, not to our past.
My love belongs to you, my beautiful Princess.

I Want To Believe

I am sitting here right now, trying to figure this all out.
I want you to know, what my confusion is all about.

My body is shackling, I can't stop the pain.
My mind is shattered, my heart is the same.

I want so much, to believe everything you say.
Each time I have trusted, you hurt me the same way.

I keep trying to forgive, because of what's in my heart.
I always have this feeling, of my soul being torn apart.

Ripped to shreds, and then thrown on hell's fire.
By you my love, the one I desire.

All the goodness and love, everything I hold dear.
I cry out in pain, but you refuse to hear.

You tell me that you love me, you want for me to stay.
Then you always hurt me, and start pushing me away.

Each time my forgiveness, is much harder to achieve.
I hope someday soon, you will also start to believe.

I believe in our love, and I believe in what is right.
I want so much to believe in you, My Princess in the Night.

Joseph A. Howard
07/28/2018

I dedicate this poem to you my Princess.

My love is about, the only thing I have left.
Your knife I can feel, it is still in my chest.

My blood is flowing, out onto the ground.
You tell me to get up, stop lying around.

Hurry up and forgive me, what's taking you so long?
Why don't you trust me? I've done nothing wrong.

What I Want

What I want, is to have a normal day.
Not having to fear, the things that you might say.

I know you see things differently, than other people see.
You just can't understand, how much you're hurting me.

I try to be understanding, and to look the other way.
For some things that you have done, it is me that has to pay.

I hope you soon will see, that we are part of each other.
The things you often do, makes me want to shudder.

I want to see you smile, and be happy every day.
I'm doing everything I can, please don't push me away.

I wish I knew, what to do, to ignite our love again.
To get back to how it was, when our love had first began.

I want to do, all that you do, for someone that you love.
To hold you tight, and let you know, you are my one beloved.

I want for us to have our peace, and a truly wonderful life.
To be happy together, for many years, with you there as my wife.

I want so much to be assured, that our light will shine so bright.
What I want, is to be with you, My Princess in the Night.

Joseph A. Howard
07/29/2018

I dedicate this poem to you my love.

There was a time when we were truly in love.
I remember seeing the spark in your eyes.
And I will never forget how I felt.
I want to see the love in your eyes again.

I want to feel your love again.
I want you to be happy again.
I love you.

Fading

My beautiful princess, where have you gone?
I have been searching for you, for far too long.

Why did you give up, and just walk away.
My princess come back, I want you to stay.

I feel so alone, my light is starting to fade.
My life is now loneliness, I wish that you had stayed.

The demons in the darkness, now coming ever closer.
I need you to find me, before the darkness takes me over.

My light is ever fading, I fear that it is out.
The demons come closer, my will I'm starting to doubt.

Will I survive this horrible fight? Without you by my side.
I have lost my will without you here, nothing left inside.

I no longer want to live this life, so abandoned and alone.
My legs give out and I collapse, to the coldness of the stone.

As the darkness closes in, I can feel the demon's breath.
Not much longer must I wait, till I feel its kiss of death.

With the end now so close, all I can think about is you.
I remember you said you love me, my love I love you too.

My beautiful princess you saved my life, why did you leave me here?
I have suffered and endured all this pain, still living my biggest fear.

Through the last flicker of my light, I can just barely see.
That you have become my demon, the one who's attacking me.

My love, my life, my beautiful wife, dear God, what have you become?
The poison's flowing through your veins, to this demon you have succumb.

You never left me like I thought you had, you have always been here too.
My beautiful princess my biggest fear, now I see it's you.

The demon's kiss has taken you away, its poison is so strong.
Should I give in to be with you, my love it won't be long.

I have thought about, how it would be, to just give in to its kiss.
My love for you is more than I can bear, please don't let me do this.

There must be a way for you to come back, from darkness into the light.
Dear God I pray please bring her back, My Princess in the Night.

Joseph A. Howard
07/30/2018

I dedicate this poem to the demon I love.
My love, I would do anything to be with you. Even become a demon myself,
if that's what you want me to do.
I love you.

Broken

All the pain and suffering, everything that I feel.
You want me to forgive you, but give no time to heal.

It will take some time, to get over what you've done.
The hurt that I'm feeling, will take some time to overcome.

I wish it was as easy, as you think that it should be.
My emotions run much deeper, I wish that you could see.

If you could then you would know, the passion that I feel.
The pain I have inside my head, will take some time to heal.

I know that it's not easy, to see what you have done.
For me it's just as hard, to see what I've become.

The pain that you are feeling, you want to put it behind.
Your pain is from your conscience, it's not the same as mine.

Mine is from the heart, it takes much more time to heal.
You want to believe that it's me, that I'm broken because I feel.

I was not broken, before you did what you did.
Now I am lying on the ground, crying like a kid.

Not believing, what you did was wrong, will never make it right.
I was not the broken one, My Princess in the Night.

Joseph A. Howard
07/30/2018

I dedicate this poem to you my love.

My dearest princess, my love, I have been broken many times before,
completely destroyed a few.
It took many years to put myself back together.
When we met, I was fragile, but whole.

Yes, I was covered with cracks and the love that I used as the glue, to glue myself back together, was not the strongest.

I know how it feels to be broken.

I hope that our love for each other will be the glue that will heal us, and be strong enough to keep us together forever.

I love you my princess.

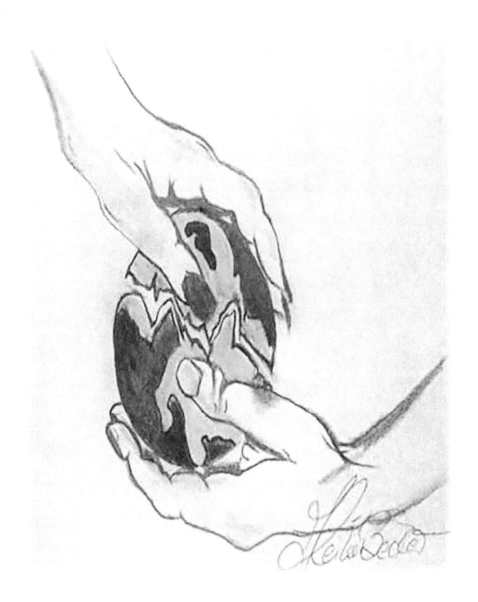

Hold On

Anything is possible, if you hold on and believe.
Never letting go, having faith you will achieve.

The things you will do, to find out who you are.
Just look inside your heart, your future's not that far.

Look inside and you will see, that things are getting better.
The more you look, the more you'll see, your life is coming together.

You have to hold on, if you want to survive, recovery is what you need,
Filling your life, with love and hope, it's your soul that you have to feed.

Take my love, and hold it close, put it into your heart.
Think about the end, before you ever think about the start.

Some things we do in the moment, might seem like there all right.
Not everything that happens in life, is always so black and white.

The choices that we make, reflect on how we see.
The life that were living, and how hard this life should be.

Hold on my love, to who you are, and all your hopes and dreams.
Things are never, really as bad, as bad as everything seems.

Hold on and believe, that our future can be bright.
When we hold onto each other, My Princess in the Night.

Joseph A. Howard
08/05/2018

I dedicate this poem to you my Love.

Things have been hard, but I never let my love go.
My Princess hold on, and let's go with the flow.

The Battle Rages On

The battle rages on, deep inside my head.
I will keep on fighting, until the day that I am dead.

The demon that's inside me, that I have loved for so long.
Has destroyed my life so much, now I want it to be gone.

The battle to decide, over who will control my mind.
Will it be me or my demon, I will no longer be confined.

This battle is eternal, it can never ever be won.
This demon of addiction, took me from my son.

Controlling this demon, who has caused me so much pain.
As the battle rages on inside, I'm not fighting this in vain.

There are so many reasons, to keep fighting this good fight.
I remember every one of them, as I kiss them all goodnight.

It hides inside the darkness, where no one else can see.
All the pain that it causes, and the scars it's left in me.

The battle rages on, deep within my soul.
Constantly fighting back, so it can never take control.

My life is mine to live, you cannot take it away.
I'm living in the light now, and that's where I want to stay.

A life full of love, where everything feels so good.
To feel my true emotions, like I know I always should.

There will be pain and heartache, all of this I know.
It's all part of being alive, and now I'm loving it so.

No more in the darkness, I want to live life in the light.
The battle rages on inside, your Princess in the Night.

Joseph A. Howard
08/22/2018

Sunrise

When God made you, he instantly new.
Everything, would be brightened by you.

The very first day, that you opened your eyes.
The sun came out, and filled the skies.

That was the day, that you started to shine.
Before your smile, was the darkest of time.

My life was so gray, no more love for me.
I tried to look happy, just for others to see.

My life was so empty, no reason to go on.
My emotions locked away, everything was gone.

I locked them away, deep inside my mind.
I did not want to feel, so I left them confined.

The key to my heart, I kept hidden from all.
Too much pain, each time that I would fall.

Then came the day, you came into my life.
I felt the sunrise, your warmth was so rife.

I gave you the key, that I have guarded for so long.
So you can unlock the door, to enter where you belong.

You opened the door, and let my love run free.
So much more, than you ever thought there could be.

The wave of love, that came through that door.
So much all at once, it knocked you to the floor.

It took a little time, to get back on your feet.
My love is strong, my emotions so deep.

The feelings that I feel, my love is so intense.
It cannot be controlled, there is no defense.

My heart is on fire, and it's burning for you.
I know my love is real, I hope that yours is too.

When I look into your eyes, I can see all your love,
I know in my heart, you were sent from above.

This feeling of love, you brought back into my life.
Now my new love, has replaced all my strife.

The grayness around me, now full color in your light.
You are my sunrise, My Princess in the Night.

Joseph A. Howard
08/26/2018

I dedicate this poem to the light of my life. My sunshine,
You brought back the light of love into my life.
I Love You My Princess.

Family

You and me, together combined.
The strongest union, you'll ever find.

A source of love, and a source of hope.
It's the source of everything, we need to cope.

It's the strength from our love, that we need to overcome.
Discarded at first, but to this love we have succumbed.

My love my life, I cherish you every day.
I thank our dear Lord, that he sent you my way.

A connection like ours, is not easy to find.
The stars above, must have all been aligned.

For something so special, so true and devout.
Feeling everything, there's no longer any doubt.

Our future has been written, our love is meant to be.
Not everyone around us, can see what we can see.

Until they do, we must hold on to our love.
We pray to God, he might give them a little shove.

Until everyone can see, to our love we must stay true.
No matter what may happen, my love is here for you.

There have been angry words, spoken out of fear.
For us to move forward, our decision must be clear.

Family is so precious, we should try to make it work.
There are others involved, that we do not want to hurt.

The forgiveness that we need, we can find within our hearts.
Before it goes any further, I pray the forgiveness starts.

Healing is a feeling, that we should always try to share.
To overcome all the hurt, and the feelings of despair.

Family is too important, I no longer want to fight.
I love you too much, My Princess in the Night.

Joseph A. Howard
08/27/2018

I dedicate this poem to my family.
You are my family.
I love you my Princess

The Pain Inside

The pain inside, is more than I can hide, I feel like I'm crashing.
Every time I start to feel, I get another bashing.

No time to heal, or even catch my breath.
Sometimes I feel, I'm getting closer to death.

The ups and downs, that I feel every day.
The pain in my mind, that will not go away.

The darkness is around me, I can see no more light.
I no longer even know, if I want to win this fight.

The struggles in my life, are getting harder every day.
I am not really sure, if I should try to even stay?

Is this life worth, all the pain that I must live?
Or should I give up? I have nothing more to give.

It's getting harder to face, every morning that I see.
I have no more trust, not even trust in me.

I know I will fail, and hurt those that I love.
I am standing on a cliff, please just give me a shove.

To end this life, of all this torture and shame.
This addiction is not mine, but I feel its pain.

Do I want to keep living, constantly fighting this fight?
All the pain inside me, My Princess in the Night.

Joseph A. Howard
08/28/2018

I dedicate this poem to you my love,
Sometimes I struggle with my emotions too.

These are the feelings, that I try to hide.
They are how I feel, deep down inside.
The pain that is there, it will not subside.
Believe me my love, I have already tried.

Everything I live for, is causing me pain.
Sometimes I feel, that I must be insane.
Love is so hard, are my struggles in vain?
Death is at my door, am I happy he came?

New Beginning

New beginnings are not easy, there are so many things to do.
The only thing that helps me, is knowing I'm with you.

When everything seems to just go wrong, and nothing will go right.
When we feel so overwhelmed, that we cannot sleep at night.

If it's not one thing, then it is another, life keeps knocking us down.
We try to count our blessings, but nothing can be found.

When everything's in shambles, there's only one thing left to do.
Try to find another way, to a new beginning for me and you.

Stop for a moment and look around, look at all we've done.
Look at all the things we do, do you really call this fun?

The choices we make, every day, not always the best for us.
The road that we've been going down, this direction we must discuss.

Sometimes in life, we just have to stop, to figure out what we want.
The decisions we make, affect our lives, our fate we should not taunt.

By changing what we do, we can change to a new direction.
If we start within our love? Then were starting with perfection.

The past is the past, so we put it behind, never looking back.
There is a new life, for us at hand, if we stay on the right track.

Yes it's scary, I know this is true, not knowing what will be.
Put your faith, in our love, so your future stays with me.

We try to keep, our love so pure, and our devotion oh so strong.
We use our love, as a faithful guide, so nothing can go wrong.

A leap of faith, is all it takes, to start our new life right.
A new beginning, for me and you, My Princess in the Night.

Joseph A. Howard
08/29/2018

I dedicate this poem to our love, a love that is so true.
Starting over again, a new beginning for me and you.

I Love You

Lost

I am feeling so very lost, deep inside my mind.
I don't know what to do? It's my love I cannot find.

I am frantically searching, to find what I have lost.
To feel it one more time, no matter what the cost.

I know my love is here, I would never throw it away.
It's lost inside my mind, I keep searching every day.

Did I put it over here? Behind my pain and fear?
Or is it behind this bottle? That is holding my last tear.

Maybe it was taken, and given to someone else.
Just the very thought of this, my soul begins to melt.

It can't be lost, it must be here.
My love is gone, nothing is clear.

Desperation takes control, there's nothing I can do.
Searching through my mind, I haven't got a clue.

Where did I put it, oh where can it be?
My light is slowly fading, it's getting hard to see.

Can you help me find it? There's nothing left in sight.
Did I give it all to you? My Princess in the Night.

Joseph A. Howard
09/05/2018

I dedicate this poem to the love I thought I lost.

I found it in you.
I love you so much my beautiful princess.

Death and Destruction

Death and destruction, as far as the eye can see.
The corpses of my emotions, that this demon took from me.

Lies and deception, are the weapons that it used.
The loss of my emotions, has left me so confused.

My psyche has been broken, shattered once again.
I fear it might be broken, until my mortal end.

As I search for my emotions, no place left for me to hide.
Pain and fear are all that's left, the demon is still inside.

This demon that I love, that I brought into my mind.
You promised not to hurt me, how could I be so blind.

My emotions are now gone, my mind has been destroyed.
The only place that I felt safe, now I must avoid.

To rebuild my mind will take some time, that's if I ever can.
Things like this are deadly, it's this demon's evil plan.

You came to me my princess, to help me win my fight.
You turned into my demon, My Princes in The Night.

Joseph A. Howard
09/06/2018

I dedicate this poem to the demon that I love.
Please come back into the light.

Redemption

My love for you is endless, redemption will always be here.
You gave into the demon's kiss, and became my biggest fear.

I beg of you, my princess, please stop with your attack.
Take my heart and my hand, let me show you the way back.

The demon's kiss is poison, you will always lose your way.
Love is never easy, once you've been led astray.

I know that I am broken, just not the same as you.
We can rebuild each other, our love can be the glue.

It will not be easy, to overcome this demon's hold.
The battles we must fight, will leave us feeling cold.

This fight will never be over, it will be our eternal chore.
This demon will always be lurking, just outside the door.

I will be here to help you, every single day.
You do not have to worry, my love I'm here to stay.

Always look to the future, don't ever try to look back.
If you look it in the eyes, the demon will attack.

Some of your friends, are still dancing its evil dance.
Until they are ready, you cannot take the chance.

They will tell you they are finished, playing with that life.
You must be very careful, they could have a hidden knife.

This demon is so evil, turning your love into all lies.
It will show up like an angel, then change before your eyes.

Once you have been bitten, this demon will take control.
Infecting every part of you, right down into your soul.

My dearest love, I do not want, to leave you all alone.
One thing that this demon fears, when love becomes your home.

Love can take this demon's curse, and rip it all to shreds.
Love for another in your heart, is what this demon dreads.

Take my hand and walk with me, down this path of light.
Redemption is waiting here for you, My Princess in the Night.

Joseph A. Howard
09/07/2018

I dedicate this poem to you my princess.

We can find our way back.
With love anything is possible.
I love you my princess.

Decisions

The biggest step you will ever take, is deciding to walk away.
To leave that life behind you, when part of you wanted to stay.

The choices we make determine our life, your future is at stake.
The decision you made was so hard, but you know it's no mistake.

It is not going to be easy, to leave everything you know.
You thought of every reason, before you decided to go.

The journey that you are taking, to a new life that lies ahead.
Not knowing where you're going, it's not the future that you dread.

This path that you are taking, you know it's for the best.
Don't worry about what happened, our love will pass the test.

Know that I will be waiting, once you find your way.
No matter what may happen, tomorrow's a better day.

Just put the past behind you, never forgetting why you left.
Keep those reasons with you, I know you'll do what's best.

Now your life is changing, getting easier every day.
You're looking to the future, to the new life on its way.

Your past is now behind you, you vow to stay on track.
Just keep going where you're going, no reason to look back.

This decision that you made, turned your darkness into light.
Some decisions can be good for you, My Princess in the Night.

Joseph A. Howard
09/08/2018
I dedicate this poem to the strongest and most amazing woman I know.
I love you for making this decision.
You will have the life that you always wanted.

Step By Step

Now that rehab's over, you are finally coming home.
Remember my sweet princess, you don't have to do it alone.

Step by step we take this on, we will conquer every day.
I will always be here, to help you find a better way.

I know that it's not easy, but you know it must be done.
The cravings that you're feeling, this battle can be won.

Count on me to be here, to give you what you need.
With my loving arms around you, I know you will succeed.

I can sense that you are worried, your fear is all too real.
I know that you're uneasy, you can feel the fear I feel.

Try my love to understand, my fear is not what you think.
My fear is that I will fail you, or push you to the brink.

I know I can be overwhelming, and my love can be too much.
I want to be everything you need, to heal you with my touch.

You might think I want perfection, but all I want is you.
I want you to be happy, but sometimes I will overdo.

Nothing has to be perfect, we just have to be all right.
Step by step we got this, My Princess in the Night.

Joseph A. Howard
09/11/2018

I dedicate this poem to my biggest fear,
That I will not be enough, or too much.
Please forgive me if I screw up,
I don't want to hurt you, I Love You.

Where Are You

My beautiful princess, where have you gone.
I am sitting here asking, what I did wrong.

I know you have been struggling, every single day.
I am doing all I can, to help you find your way.

The feeling of being trapped, in a life you think can't last.
So you think about the one, the one you left in the past.

The past you had was toxic, I don't know why you look back.
Nothing there is helpful, you were always being attacked.

Or do you not remember, all the pain you have endured.
Almost losing everything, your destruction was assured.

Where are you my princess? I can't sense you anymore.
This link that we've been sharing, it's like you closed the door.

I know you have your fears, about everything right now.
It will all get better, if you could only just see how.

I take my love and all my trust, and I give it all to you.
I think sometimes you can't understand, this is what lovers do.

To you this must be frightening, to put your trust in me.
My love it's only normal, I wish that you could see.

Put your faith in my love, and do not be afraid.
I will be here waiting, I wish that you had stayed.

Please my love come back to me, do not lose your fight.
Where are you my only love, My Princess in the Night.
Joseph A. Howard
09/29/2018

I dedicate this poem to you my love.
I miss you so much.
Just please come back home, we need you.

I Cannot Say Goodbye

The darkness that surrounds me, I have nothing left inside.
My life I fear is over, since they told me that you died.

The pain that I am feeling, will never go away.
Why did you have to do this? There is always another way.

No kiss goodbye not even a hug, you were not even home.
My love my life you left me, sitting here all alone.

The knock on the door at 3am, to tell me you were gone.
They say they found your body, unconscious on the lawn.

They tried their best to save you, but there was nothing they could do.
There must be some mistake, there's no way it can be you.

I cannot say goodbye, I love you way too much.
I cannot go on living, knowing I'll never feel your touch.

Why my dearest princess, did you ever start again?
Your son and I were here for you, how hard it must have been.

To come to us instead the others, to find a different way.
My sweet love I can't understand, why you couldn't stay.

The fact that you were struggling, you never should have hid.
There is no shame in asking for help, my love I wish you did.

Things will always get better, no matter what went wrong.
I wish it could have been enough, just knowing you belong.

Now were left here hurting, my desire is hard to fight.
I cannot say goodbye to you, My Princess in the Night.

Joseph A. Howard
09/30/2018

Why my sweet princess, Why?
I love you and I miss you so much.

Beyond The End

I will love you beyond the end, after my last breath.
I want so much to be with you, to join you with my death.

My love my life is meaningless, without you by my side.
My life will soon be over, no more pain for me to hide.

The demon that finally took you, I curse it every day.
Now it's time to be with you, our love will find a way.

This demon of addiction, that took you away from me.
It cannot stop our love, because our love is meant to be.

I wish we had more time, to share our life together.
Now in death we will be, side by side forever.

I cannot wait to be with you, I miss you way too much.
I cannot live without you, never feeling your tender touch.

To those I leave behind, do not grieve for me.
I am going to join my love, it's where I want to be.

I feel like I am floating, no longer in my space.
Take my hand and hold me, so we stay in the same place.

Up or down I do not care, as long as I'm with you.
It doesn't matter where you go, I want to be there too.

Soon we'll be together, then we can walk into the light.
Love that lasts beyond the end, My Princess in the Night.

Joseph A. Howard
09/31/2018
Good bye everyone,
Hello my princess,
Love that lasts beyond the end.